Developing Literacy
SPEAKING & LISTENING

PHOTOCOPIABLE ACTIVITIES
FOR THE LITERACY HOUR

year

6

Ray Barker and
Christine Moorcroft

Contents

Drama

Acknowledgements
Every effort has been made to trace copyright holders and to obtain their permission for use of copyright material. The authors and publishers would be pleased to rectify in future editions any error or omission.

Published 2005 by A & C Black Publishers Limited
38 Soho Square, London W1D 3HB
www.acblack.com

ISBN-10: 0-7136-7374-5
ISBN-13: 978-0-7136-7374-6

Copyright text © Ray Barker, 2005
Copyright illustrations © Pat Murray, 2005
Copyright cover illustration © Andy Robb, 2005
Editor: Lucy Poddington
Designer: Heather Billin

The authors and publishers would like to thank Fleur Lawrence and Kim Perez for their advice in producing this series of books.

A CIP catalogue record for this book is available from the British Library.

Printed and bound in Great Britain by Cromwell Press Ltd, Trowbridge, Wiltshire.

A & C Black uses paper produced with elemental chlorine-free pulp, harvested from managed sustainable forests.

Introduction

Developing Literacy: Speaking and Listening is a series of seven photocopiable activity books for the Literacy Hour. Each book provides a range of speaking and listening activities and supports the teaching and learning objectives identified in *Curriculum Guidance for the Foundation Stage* and by the Primary National Strategy in *Speaking, Listening, Learning: working with children in Key Stages 1 and 2*.

Speaking and listening skills are vital to children's intellectual and social development, particularly in helping them to:

- develop creativity;
- interact with others;
- solve problems;
- speculate and discourse;
- form social relationships;
- build self-confidence.

The activities in this book focus on the following four aspects of speaking and listening:

- **Speaking:** being able to speak clearly; developing and sustaining ideas in talk
- **Listening:** developing active listening strategies; using skills of analysis
- **Group discussion and interaction:** taking different roles in groups; working collaboratively; making a range of contributions
- **Drama:** improvisation; working in role; scripting and performing; responding to performances

Using the activity sheets

The materials show how speaking and listening can be relevant to all parts of literacy lessons, in whole-class work, in group or paired work, during independent work and in plenary sessions. The activities encourage the inclusion of all learners, since talking and contributing to group work are often more accessible than writing for lower-achieving children and for those who speak English as an additional language.

Extension activities

Most of the activity sheets end with a challenge (**Now try this!**), which reinforces and extends the children's learning and provides the teacher with an opportunity for assessment. These more challenging activities might be appropriate for only a few children; it is not expected that the whole class should complete them. For most of the extension activities, the children will need a notebook or a separate sheet of paper.

Organisation

Few resources are needed besides scissors, glue, word banks and simple dictionaries. Access to ICT resources – computers, video, tape recorders – will also be useful at times. To help teachers select appropriate learning experiences for their pupils, the activities are grouped into sections within the book. The pages need not be presented in the order in which they appear, unless stated otherwise. The sheets are intended to support, rather than direct, the teacher's planning.

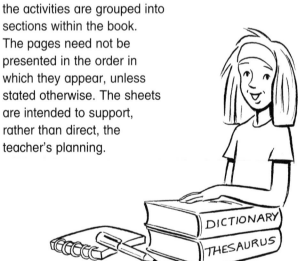

Brief notes are provided at the bottom of each page, giving ideas and suggestions for making the most of the activity sheet. They may include suggestions for a whole-class introduction, a plenary session or follow-up work using an adapted version of the activity sheet. These notes may be masked before photocopying if desired. More detailed notes and suggestions can be found on pages 6–9.

Effective group work

Many of the activities involve children working in groups. Here are some ideas to consider as you prepare for group work.

Before you start

HOW?

- How are deadlines and groupings made clear to groups?
- How might different children undertake different tasks?
- How will you organise time and space to give children the opportunity to rehearse and practise new skills?
- How will the children reflect on what they have learned about talk and its impact?

WHEN?

- When is working in a group appropriate?
- When is speaking and listening to be the focus of an activity?
- When is speaking and listening the outcome?
- When is it right for one child to become 'an expert' and inform others?

WHERE?

- Where in the class is the work going to take place in order to give space and manage noise levels?
- Where is it best for you to be to monitor the groups?
- Where might group work result in a finished product, such as a leaflet, and what resources will you need?

Tips for grouping children

- Be clear about the nature and purpose of the task.
- Decide which type of grouping is best for your purpose (pairs, attainment groups, friendship groups).
- Consider the advantages of mixed- or single-sex groupings in your particular class.
- Consider how you will include all abilities in these groups.
- Think carefully about who will lead groups and how you can vary this.
- Aim to vary the experience for the children: for example, using different groupings, ways of recording or learning environments. Experiment with what works best for different kinds of learners.

Your role

The notes in this book suggest an active role for you as a teacher, and give examples of how you can develop children's learning. Your role will vary from activity to activity, but here are some general points to bear in mind when working with children on speaking and listening activities:

- Be challenging in your choice of topics.
- Don't be afraid to use the correct language for talk: for example, *dialogue, gesture, narrator, negotiate, open and closed questions* and so on.
- Set the ground rules: everyone has a right to speak but everyone also has a duty to listen to others, take turns and so on.
- Move around to monitor what is happening in the groups. You can move on group discussions by developing and questioning what the children say.
- Provide models of the patterns of language expected for particular kinds of speech.
- Try to steer children away from using closed questions.
- Ensure children give extended answers and always ask them to explain their thinking.
- Allow children time to formulate their responses and treat everyone's responses with respect – but avoid praising every answer.

Assessment

An assessment sheet is provided on page 48 for children to assess their own progress. The children can complete the sheet on their own or in discussion with you. It is not expected that you will be able to assess the entire class at any one time. It is best to focus on a small group of children each week, although whole-class monitoring may be possible with certain activities, such as drama activities where children perform to the whole class.

Other activities in the book are ideal for the collection of evidence over the year (for example, *Persuade me, Be safe!, Why save water?, Note it!, Rescue mission, Character lines, Tense moments*) and for children to assess one another's skills in speaking and listening (*A good argument, Debate it, No words needed, Firework sense, I want some more...*). All the information should be assimilated for an end-of-year summary to facilitate target setting and the transition to Year 7.

Notes on the activities

Speaking

The activities in this section provide contexts to encourage the children to use a range of oral techniques, such as speaking persuasively and holding the audience's attention through style of delivery. There are opportunities to plan for a whole-class debate and to use language and role-play to explore ideas.

Don't say it! (page 10). This activity encourages the children to think about what they say and the effect on the listener. The phrases all contain redundant (unnecessary) words: for example, there are no degrees of uniqueness, so it is not possible to be 'almost unique'. This should give rise to some interesting discussion and will help children to reflect on the words they use in making their own arguments.

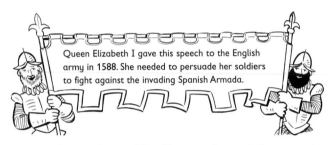

Queen Elizabeth I gave this speech to the English army in 1588. She needed to persuade her soldiers to fight against the invading Spanish Armada.

Persuade me (page 11). After reading out the speech, draw attention to the way Elizabeth I flatters her 'faithful and loving people' and reminds her audience of soldiers that even though she is 'a weak and feeble woman', she herself will take up arms. Note also the references to God, as if God is on the side of the English. You could show the children well-known speeches from Shakespeare's *Henry V* which use the same techniques (for example, the speech beginning 'Once more unto the breech dear friends…'). The passage on this activity sheet could also be used for practice in highlighting key points.

A good argument (page 12). This reinforces the concept of an 'argument' as a rational and constructive speech intended to persuade someone. Remind the children that an argument does not involve shouting! You may need to explain concepts such as thinking of objections that others may make and preparing counter-arguments. Discuss the use of gestures, reminding the children that confidence and use of body language is key to making a point (see also page 22).

Be safe! (page 13). This provides a useful framework to scaffold a persuasive argument. The framework can be used in many other written and spoken contexts. Before the children give their speeches, remind them of techniques for holding the audience's attention, such as making eye contact and varying the pace and volume of delivery.

Why save water? (page 14). This could be useful in a comparison of language used for different purposes. In a science report on an experiment, the writer or speaker would use precise language and would not address the audience directly; compare this with the persuasive language of an argument. You could also point out the frequent use of passive verbs in science: for example, 'the temperature was measured' rather than 'we measured the temperature'.

All about debates (page 15). In this activity the children research some of the conventions of formal debate. The questions can be answered as follows:

The **chairperson** is in charge of the debate. He or she briefly introduces the speakers and the topic of the debate, then invites each speaker in turn to give their speech. The chairperson also conducts the vote at the end of the debate.

The **timekeeper** makes sure that all the speakers speak for the same length of time. He or she should indicate to the speakers how much time they have left: for example, by banging on the table when there is one minute remaining.

One person can be chosen to take **minutes** – a written record of the main points of the debate, and its outcome.

The **proposition team** aims to persuade the audience to support the motion being debated. The **opposition team** puts forward arguments for the opposite point of view. The first speaker on each team should briefly introduce what the rest of the team are going to say, and the order of speakers.

Members of the audience have the opportunity to **'speak from the floor'**, explaining which side they support, and why. They can also ask questions which the proposition or opposition team may answer at the end.

The **order of the speakers** is usually as follows: proposition team, opposition team, members of the floor, opposition summary speaker, proposition summary speaker.

The **vote** is taken once all the speeches have been made.

Debate it (page 16). This activity helps the children to prepare for a formal debate. It will be helpful if they first complete the activity on page 15. You could debate a school-related topic, such as 'Part of the playground should be set aside for skateboarding.' Alternatively, you could choose a topic from history and invite the children to give their speeches in role. An example from 19th-century history might be 'Parliament must introduce laws to stop children being badly treated at work.'

Question time (page 17). This provides an opportunity for the children to carry out role-play interviews with fictional characters they know well. The children take on defined roles and should be able to support one another. If possible, let the children watch a recorded television interview with a famous person before they begin, encouraging them to make notes about the kinds of questions asked. They should also study how the interviewer reshapes questions when necessary.

In a dilemma (page 18). Discuss dilemmas from books the children have read, and model how a character in a dilemma might argue with him- or herself about the pros and cons of possible courses of action. The children's role-plays should stimulate class discussion of the issues raised, with other children being able to comment on the broader issues even if they have not read the book themselves.

Discuss this and **Who is right?** (pages 19 and 20). These activities focus on personal and social issues which have no 'right answer' and should be looked at from different points of view. When discussing viewpoints as a class, try to ensure that all the children are involved and feel secure enough to express their ideas freely.

Listening

These activities encourage sustained listening in order to identify ways of communicating effectively using an appropriate level of formality. There are also activities which help the children to make effective notes when listening.

Tongue in a twist (page 21). This activity helps the children to realise that speaking and listening are interconnected, and that in order to communicate effectively they need to listen to themselves and really think about what they are saying. The tongue-twisters could also be useful for revising word-level objectives about the sounds of words and their different spellings.

No words needed (page 22). Non-verbal communication is an important part of speaking and listening and the children need to be aware of its importance in conveying meaning and mood. This activity could be linked with role-play and drama activities, such as *Freeze!* on page 42.

Fraffly well spoken (pages 23). These are humorous examples of how spoken words in a particular accent can be written down to convey the pronunciation. The writer, Afferbeck Lauder, uses standard forms of English in a non-standard way, by making

'upper class English' into a kind of dialect. Talk about how you have to listen to an accent before it can be imitated. Discuss how, when speaking Fraffly, you can use gesture, expression and tone of voice to make yourself easily understood. 'Translations' are as follows: *Thank you; Frightfully nice of you; I quite agree; Westminster Abbey is in London; Let us go to Regents Park; Who is Gregory? Or George? Or Simon?; Have you seen Emily?; I do the following at school: painting, poetry, drama.* The conversation in the extension activity is set in the context of a shop and reads: *'Sorry Madam. Afraid we can't help you.' 'Thank you'. 'Good afternoon madam.'*

The Crystal Palace and **Note it!** (pages 24 and 25). These activities offer an opportunity to revise the features of notes and the difference between making notes for yourself to refer to, and making notes for someone else to understand. The children are encouraged to consider the audience and purpose of their note-making. Features of the notes on page 24 include abbreviations and the omission of words such as 'the', 'it' and some verbs. Check that the children understand all the abbreviations used in the passage.

A Scottish ballad (page 26). This ballad uses dialect words and also links with text-level objectives on poetic form. Read the poem to the children or find a suitable recording to ensure that the sound is as authentic as possible. It is important that this activity is not used to make fun of an accent. Ensure that the children understand the difference between dialect and accent. A dialect is a form of slang used in a town or region, and uses some non-standard English words. Accent is the way in which words are pronounced. Many of the words will be understood when read aloud, although they may appear to be unfamiliar on the page; this is an interesting discussion point and can link with word-level objectives.

Talk proper! (page 27). Here the children consider examples of formal and informal language and when it is considered appropriate to use each. This should be linked with text-level work on audience and purpose in written style. Discuss how the children can tell which phrases are formal and which are informal, drawing attention to features such as contractions (*I'd, I'll*), abbreviations (*Em*), passive verbs (*are served*), formal vocabulary (*refreshments, sufficient resources*), slang (*mate, oi*) and non-standard English (*catch you later*).

Group discussion and interaction

These activities aim to stimulate discussion but also help teachers to focus on other key areas such as how children can work together in groups to criticise constructively and respond to criticism. There are activities in which the children are required to cope with disagreement and find ways to reach a consensus within the group. Role-plays and examples of spoken language provide opportunities for the children to explore variation in language according to context and purpose.

The same but different (page 28). This links with word- and text-level objectives, and provides an opportunity for the children to work together on a research activity using a variety of media. Stress that there is no 'correct answer', but that all members of the group should offer their ideas to help the others improve their explanations. The children could use the words in example sentences to aid their explanations.

Firework sense (page 29). Here the children work in a group to plan and give a presentation on using fireworks safely. They will need to find ways of coping with disagreement so that the discussion can proceed. You may wish to organise groups so that all children in the class feel confident enough to contribute. You may also need to help groups manage their discussions so that the planning is completed within the time available.

Recycling plastic (page 30). This links with text-level work on the characteristics of explanation texts and the features of instructions. The children need to see the importance of questioning and doubting each other until they are sure they understand how plastic is recycled. They then work as a group to explain the process together. If possible, arrange for the children to present their explanations to another class, and invite audience feedback on how well the process was explained.

Back to front (page 31). The sentences in this activity are palindromes, that is, phrases which read the same when the letters are read in reverse order. The children are encouraged to seek clarification from each other and to negotiate successfully as a group.

True or false? (page 32). In this activity the children discuss statements in groups, explaining whether they think the statements are true or false. There are no right or wrong answers, so there is likely to be disagreement within the group which needs to be resolved in the extension activity. Ensure that all the children are given the opportunity to speak. During the plenary, encourage the children to reflect on the language they used to reach a consensus. You could ask them for other statements which are difficult to prove or disprove.

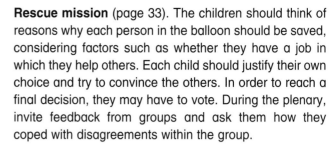

Rescue mission (page 33). The children should think of reasons why each person in the balloon should be saved, considering factors such as whether they have a job in which they help others. Each child should justify their own choice and try to convince the others. In order to reach a final decision, they may have to vote. During the plenary, invite feedback from groups and ask them how they coped with disagreements within the group.

Phone talk and **Changing audience** (pages 34 and 35). In these activities the children are encouraged to identify the ways language varies according to context and purpose. The four situations on page 34 involve speaking to different audiences: an adult who is familiar; an adult who is a stranger; a friend; and the police. You may wish to link this to speaking activities about language variation (see pages 26–27). Encourage the children to identify differences between formal and informal speech: for example, slang, dialect expressions, contractions, exclamations, use of non-standard English.

Drama

The activities in this section use a range of techniques to explore character, tension and themes in shared texts or dramatic performances. The children explore the features of films and plays, and plan their own performances for specific audiences. The activities on pages 37–39 should be used in conjunction with each other, to analyse aspects of a live or recorded performance.

Camera… action! (page 36). This activity looks at storyboarding, or using still images from a film to tell a story. There is no 'right answer' and the children should be able to arrange the pictures in a variety of ways. This is an interesting way to revise story structure and to consider how to start a narrative, how much information your audience needs and how much information you have to give to 'fill the gaps' between different parts of the story.

Character lines (page 37). In this activity the children 'grade' characters in a play or film on their various characteristics. This provides the children with a visual record of how they feel about characters. If you watch a film with the class, you could pause it at a suitable moment and ask the children to complete the character lines. Then repeat the activity at the end of the film to encourage the children to think about how their opinions have changed.

Character detective (page 38). Here the children investigate one character in depth, using evidence from the play or film to project answers to questions about the character. Ensure that the children justify their answers with reference to things the character says or does. The children could use this questioning technique to create and develop their own characters for stories.

Tense moments (page 39). This activity links with text-level objectives about story structure. If you are studying a film, it is useful to stop the film at moments of tension and ask the children questions about what is happening and how the author has made the scene as dramatic as possible. Ask the children how they think the characters will behave, then continue watching the film to see if their predictions are correct. For the extension activity, remind the children that when writing a playscript they should include information about the setting as well as stage directions to help the actors convey appropriate feelings and emotions when performing the scene. This sheet could be adapted for planning written stories or longer playscripts.

Film of the book (page 40). For this activity the children watch a film based on a book they have read, and compare the two versions. Discuss with the children the aims and features of the two kinds of media, including the advantages of books over films, and vice versa. Draw out that a successful film adaptation should make the most of the film medium, rather than following the book word for word. A wide range of films could be chosen for this activity, including adaptations of the work of popular authors such as Roald Dahl.

Character alley (page 41). This drama strategy encourages the children to give opinions about characters or situations, and opens up the discussion in a non-judgemental context. The activity could be used with the passage from *Oliver Twist* on page 45. Allow time after the main activity for the children to carry out the extension activity in pairs. This technique can be used to develop scenes in the children's own writing.

Freeze! (page 42). Here the children create 'frozen pictures' (or tableaux) showing key moments of a book they are reading or have read. If you wish, you could choose a suitable passage as the focus of the activity. Encourage the children to think carefully beforehand about how each person will contribute to the overall effect of the freeze frame. Stress the importance of keeping the freeze frames still. The extension activity asks the children to reflect in role on what is taking place, considering how the characters feel at that particular moment.

In the hot seat (page 43). This looks at the drama strategy of hot-seating. You could focus on a particular scene in a book the class is reading. Arrange the children in a circle or semi-circle with the 'hot seat' either in the middle or in front. The child in the hot seat must think of what it might be like to be the character and answer the questions in role (or the teacher can choose to be in the hot seat and answer the questions). You could invite the other children to ask their  questions in role, as other characters in the book, or simply from their perspective as readers. Allow time after the main activity for the children to carry out the extension activity in pairs. Hot-seating can be carried out as group work as well as with the whole class. You could also consider putting two children in the hot seat so that they can work together to give answers.

Speak your mind (page 44). Here the children speak the thoughts of a character at a key moment in a book. This encourages the children to use their imagination and to show empathy with the characters and their situation. Once they have noted down their ideas, move around the group inviting children to speak in turn. This can be an opportunity to encourage less confident members of the group to contribute if you wish, but be prepared to pass over any children who do not want to speak. Repeat out loud important words or phrases if you are in any doubt that others can hear them. The discussion in the extension activity is an opportunity for the children to share different views of characters.

I want some more... (page 45). If you use an interactive whiteboard you could show the children a film clip of this scene to stimulate the writing of the playscript. A clip is available on the British Film Institute site at http://lean.bfi.org.uk/material.php?theme=1&title=oliver. Stop the clip to ask questions, and encourage the children to annotate the pictures to show differences between the film and the novel text. This provides an opportunity to consider what information needs to be provided when writing a playscript. The passage on this page can be used as the focus for other drama activities (see pages 41–44). If you wish to read further excerpts to the children or work on different episodes, you can access the text of *Oliver Twist* for free at the following site: http://etext.lib.virginia.edu/toc/modeng/public/DicOliv.html.

What a performance! (page 46). In this activity everyone in the group has to work together to plan a performance of a poem. Ensure that the children are aware of and enjoy the onomatopoeic words (words whose sounds echo their meaning). Discuss how they will emphasise the sound words and use actions to make the performance interesting to parents. If possible, arrange for the children to perform the poem to an audience of parents.

A terrible beast (page 47). Here the children focus on planning a performance for an audience of young children. Discuss the kind of language and concepts that a young child would understand, to enable the children to adapt their presentation accordingly.

How did you do? (page 48). This assessment sheet enables teachers and children to identify strengths and areas for improvement. The sheet is not intended for use after every activity, but should be given when it is felt appropriate. Sections not applicable to the activity can be masked.

Don't say it!

- **Work in a group. Cut out the cards.**
- **Take turns to pick a card. Make up a sentence using the phrase.**
- **Discuss with your group what is wrong with the phrase.**

almost unique	most favourite
very possible	very impossible
very essential	reversing backwards
more superior	fairly magnificent
slightly true	almost a lie

- **With your group, make up new sentences to express the same ideas in better ways.**

Teachers' note Split the class into groups of four or five and give each group a copy of this page. Ask the children to think about whether the phrases make good descriptions and if not, why not. During the plenary, talk about the redundant words in the phrases, and compare their effectiveness with the new phrases the children come up with.

**Developing Literacy
Speaking & Listening
Year 6
© A & C BLACK**

Persuade me

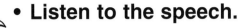

- **Listen to the speech.**

Queen Elizabeth I gave this speech to the English army in 1588. She needed to persuade her soldiers to fight against the invading Spanish Armada.

My loving people, we have been persuaded by some, that are careful of our safety, to take heed how we commit ourselves to armed multitudes, for fear of treachery; but I assure you, I do not desire to live to distrust my faithful and loving people. Let tyrants fear: I have always so behaved myself that, under God, I have placed my chiefest strength and safeguards in the loyal hearts and goodwill of my subjects. And therefore I am come amongst you at this time, not as for my recreation or sport, but being resolved, in the midst and heat of the battle, to live or die amongst you all: to lay down, for my God and for my kingdom, and for my people, my honour and my blood, even in the dust. I know I have but the body of a weak and feeble woman, but I have the heart of a king, and of a king of England, too: and think foul scorn that Parma or Spain, or any Prince of Europe, should dare to invade the borders of my realms: to which rather than any dishonour should grow by me, I myself will take up arms: I myself will be your general, judge, and rewarder of every one of your virtues in the field.

- **Underline the persuasive words and phrases in the speech.**
- **Discuss with a partner why these are persuasive.**

- **Imagine you are a soldier in 1588 who listened to this speech. In role, explain to a partner how your queen convinced you to fight.**

Teachers' note Read the passage to the children, then remind them of the historical context and discuss the language and phrases used (see page 6). Ensure the children understand the whole passage before they begin the activity.

**Developing Literacy
Speaking & Listening
Year 6
© A & C BLACK**

A good argument

- **Plan an argument on this topic.**

Work in a group of three.

Is school uniform a good idea?

- **Make notes about the main points you will make.**

1	
2	
3	
4	

- **Discuss how you can use the ideas below in your argument.**

When you present an argument:
- ☆ explain your ideas in a sensible order
- ☆ use gestures
- ☆ use examples and evidence
- ☆ stress important words and phrases
- ☆ be prepared for objections people might make.

Now try this!

- **In your group, practise and present your argument.**
- **Ask your audience how effective they think it is.**
- **Discuss ways of improving your argument.**

Teachers' note The children should first complete the activity on page 11. Split the class into groups of three and give each group a copy of this page. One child in the group should act as scribe. For the extension activity, encourage the children to listen to other groups' presentations and to comment on how effective they think they were, and why.

Developing Literacy
Speaking & Listening
Year 6
© A & C BLACK

Be safe!

- **Plan a speech to persuade children to wear seat belts in cars.**

- **Read what the law says. Think about why this is the law.**

The law
- Children aged 3–11 and under 1.5 metres in height must use an appropriate child car seat if available. Otherwise, an adult seat belt must be used if available.
- Children aged 12 or 13 and children 1.5 metres or more in height must use an adult seat belt if available.

- **Make notes to plan your speech.**

I believe that _____

because _____

_____

Furthermore, _____

_____

Surely _____

_____

Anyone can see that _____

_____

because _____

_____

The truth is _____

_____

So, it is clear that _____

- **Give your speech to the rest of the class.**

- **Make notes about what you did well and what you will do differently next time.**

Teachers' note First discuss the laws with the children and talk about the reasons behind them. Before beginning the activity, model the use of the framework and ask how many members of the class think that child safety in cars is important. After the speeches have been given, ask again. Discuss how persuasive the speeches were, and how they helped to change people's minds.

Developing Literacy
Speaking & Listening
Year 6
© A & C BLACK

Why save water?

- **You are going to plan a speech to persuade people to use less water.**

- **Here are facts on the topic. Think about how you will use them to make your point.**

- Each year about 5 million people die because they do not have enough clean water.
- Only about 3% of the world's water is fresh water. Most of this is frozen in the polar ice caps. The rest is spread unevenly across the Earth's land surface.
- Water is also used unevenly. On average, someone in the UK uses about 150 litres of water per day. Someone in Madagascar uses less than 6 litres per day.

- **Use this framework to help you plan your speech:**

I believe that

There are several reasons for this. Firstly,

Another reason is

Furthermore,

These points prove that

- **Make notes about how you will give your speech and keep your audience's attention.**

- **Then give your speech.**

- **How was your speech different from a science report on an experiment with water? Discuss it with a partner.**

Teachers' note First model the use of the framework with the children and discuss ways of holding the audience's attention when giving a speech. In the extension activity, encourage the children to think about the audience and purpose of the speech compared with the audience and purpose of a report on a science experiment.

Developing Literacy Speaking & Listening Year 6 © A & C BLACK

All about debates

- **Work in a group. Cut out the cards.**
- **The questions are all about debates. Read the cards one at a time and try to answer the questions. Make notes on the back of the cards.**

What are the duties of the chairperson?

What are the duties of the timekeeper?

What are 'minutes'?

Who are the 'proposition team' and the 'opposition team'?

What is 'speaking from the floor'?

What is the order of speakers?

When is the vote taken?

- **With your group, write a list of rules for a debate.**

Literacy
**Speaking & Listening
Year 6**
© A & C BLACK

Debate it

- **Work in a group.**
- **Use this sheet to plan what you will say in a debate.**

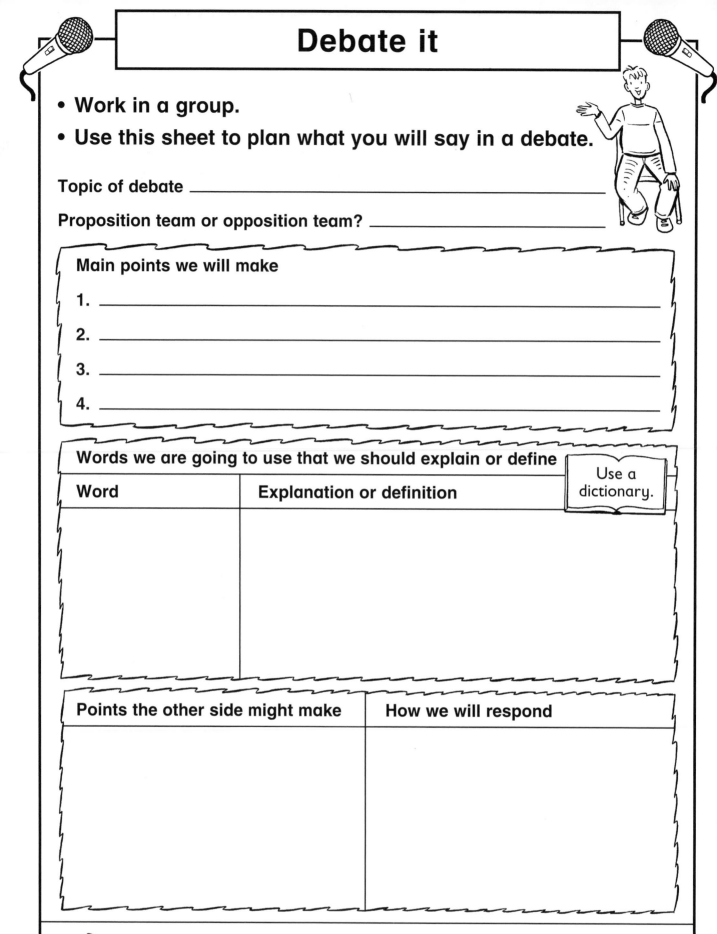

Topic of debate _____

Proposition team or opposition team? _____

Main points we will make

1. _____

2. _____

3. _____

4. _____

Words we are going to use that we should explain or define

Use a dictionary.

Word	Explanation or definition

Points the other side might make	How we will respond

- **Now decide who will say what. You could underline your main points in different colours and write a key.**

Teachers' note As a class, decide on a topic to debate (see page 6). Choose two teams of four to form the proposition and opposition teams, and elect a chairperson. Give each team a copy of this page. They should nominate one person to act as scribe. When the children have prepared their speeches, hold a formal debate.

**Developing Literacy
Speaking & Listening
Year 6
© A & C BLACK**

- **Work with a partner. Choose two characters from a book you have both read.**
- **Think of questions you could ask the characters to find out more about them. Write your questions in the speech bubbles.**

Don't write questions which can be answered 'yes' or 'no'.

Character A _____

Character B _____

- **Use your questions to role-play an interview with character A. Decide who will be the interviewer and who will be the story character.**
- **Now swap roles and role-play an interview with character B.**

Now try this!

Use formal language.

Teachers' note Give each child a copy of this page. Before the children begin, discuss types of questions and draw out that open questions are most useful in an interview situation. In the extension activity, encourage the interviewers to listen to their partner's responses and to reshape their questions when necessary.

**Developing Literacy
Speaking & Listening
Year 6
© A & C BLACK**

In a dilemma

In a dilemma, someone has to make a difficult decision about what to do.

- **Choose a dilemma from a book you have read.**
  Here are some ideas:

Should Bilbo give the Arkenstone to Bard?

The Hobbit
J R R Tolkien

Watership Down
Richard Adams

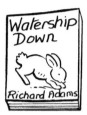

Should the rabbits trust Fiver's 'bad feeling' and leave the warren?

- **Imagine you are in the dilemma. Note down the arguments for and against each course of action.**

Book title _____

Author _____ Character _____

Possible action _____

For	Against

Possible action _____

For	Against

Now try this!

- **On your own, practise role-playing the dilemma. Argue with yourself and reach a decision about what to do.**

Teachers' note Use an example from a book that the children have just read to introduce the idea of a dilemma. Once the children have practised their role-plays, invite them to perform them to the class.

Developing Literacy
Speaking & Listening
Year 6
© A & C BLACK

Discuss this

- **Work with a partner. Choose one of these situations.**
- **Look at the problem from both points of view.**
  Discuss what should be done.

Emma is 11 and she wants a mobile phone.
Lots of her friends at school have one and
she feels left out.
Emma's parents think mobile phones are too
expensive. They tell her to wait until she is older.

Kieran is learning to play the trumpet.
He wants to give up and play football
in the park with his friends instead.
Kieran's parents want him to keep having
trumpet lessons and join a music club.

- **Make notes about your discussion.**

_____'s point of view	_____'s parents' point of view

Now try this!

- **Think of a difficult situation you have been in.**
- **Talk to a partner about how you tried to solve the problem.**

Teachers' note Give each child a copy of this page so that the children can make notes individually after their paired discussion. Stress that there is no 'right answer' to these problems, and that it is important to look at the situations from different viewpoints. Bring the whole class together to discuss the situations, ensuring that all children's ideas are respected.

Developing Literacy
Speaking & Listening
Year 6
© A & C BLACK

Who is right?

Rachid has saved up his pocket money to buy a pair of football boots like the ones his favourite player wears. His father wants him to buy a cheaper pair.

- **Should Rachid be allowed to spend his pocket money however he wants? With a partner, think of the arguments on both sides.**

Rachid's views	His father's views

Your views

I believe that _____

because _____

Although _____

I think that _____

Now try this!

- **With a partner, role-play the conversation between Rachid and his dad. Use standard English to explain your point of view.**

Teachers' note Give each child a copy of this page so that the children can make notes individually. Stress that both viewpoints need to be considered. Bring the whole class together in the plenary to discuss the situation, ensuring that all children's ideas are respected.

Developing Literacy Speaking & Listening Year 6 © A & C BLACK

Tongue in a twist

- **Imagine you are auditioning to be a presenter on children's TV. You have to perform two tongue-twisters without making a mistake!**
- **Cut out the cards. Choose two cards and practise performing them.**

Listen to each other. Think about what makes the tongue-twisters difficult to say.

A

Betty bought a bit of butter.
Betty said: 'My butter's bitter.
If I put it in my batter,
It will make my batter bitter.
Better buy some better butter.'
Betty's mother said she'd let her.
So she bought some better butter
And it made her batter better.

B

A bitter biting bittern
Bit a better brother bittern,
And the bitten better bittern
Bit the bitter biter back.
And the bitter bittern, bitten,
By the better-bitten bittern,
Said, 'I'm a bitter biter bit, alack!'

C

Mr See owned a saw.
And Mr Soar owned a see-saw.
Now See's saw sawed Soar's see-saw
Before Soar saw See,
Which made Soar sore.
Had Soar seen See's saw
Before See sawed Soar's see-saw,
See's saw would not have sawed
Soar's see-saw.

D

Silly Sally swiftly shooed seven
silly sheep.
The seven silly sheep Silly Sally
shooed shilly-shallied south.
These sheep shouldn't sleep in
a shack;
Sheep should sleep in a shed.

Now try this!

- **Find some more tongue-twisters, or make up your own. Practise performing them.**

Teachers' note Make enough copies of this page for the children to share one between two. Encourage the children to think of this as a real audition so that they rehearse properly. They should listen to themselves and consider the different effects they can create by varying the pace and volume.

**Developing Literacy
Speaking & Listening
Year 6
© A & C BLACK**

No words needed

- **Work in a group. Cut out the cards.**
- **Take turns to pick a card.**
  Discuss how you think the person is feeling. How can you tell?

A 	**B** 	**C** 
D 	**E** 	**F** 

Now try this!

- **Think about how 'body language' can show other feelings or emotions.**
- **Choose one feeling or emotion to role-play.**
  Ask your group to say how they think you are feeling.

Teachers' note Split the class into groups of four to six and give each group a copy of this page. Explain that there is no 'right answer' and the pictures could be interpreted in different ways. The pictures could be used as prompts for developing role-play.

Developing Literacy
Speaking & Listening
Year 6
© A & C BLACK

Fraffly well spoken

- **A writer has invented a new language called 'Fraffly'.**

Fraffly caned a few.

Don't mention it.

- **Work in a group. Cut out the cards.**
- **Pick a card each. On your own, practise saying the phrase.**
  Listen to yourself and try to understand it.
- **Say the phrase to the others in your group.**
  Do they understand?

Thairk yaw. *HINT: Thanks!*	Fraffly nacer few. *HINT: Most grateful*
Egg-wetter gree. *HINT: Definitely!*	Wessmin Streppy is in London. *HINT: A famous church*
Let us go to Rich in Spock. *HINT: Lots of grass*	Who is Grairgrair? Or Jodge? Or Salmon? *HINT: Boys' names*
Have you seen Airmlair? *HINT: Girl's name*	I do the following at school: penting, poitreh, drommer. *HINT: Lessons*

Now try this!

- **Role-play this conversation with a partner.**

Sorrair mottom. Fred we corn telpew.

G'doft noon, mottom.

Thairk yaw.

- **Make up your own conversation using 'Fraffly'.**

Teachers' note Split the class into groups of four to six and give each group a copy of this page. Explain to the children that when speaking the phrases they do not have to adopt an accent; they should simply speak the words as they are written and the 'Fraffly' accent will emerge. Discuss the example with them ('Frightfully kind of you'), and draw out the humour.

Developing Literacy Speaking & Listening Year 6 © A & C BLACK

The Crystal Palace

- **Read these notes about the Crystal Palace.**

Built 1851 – housed Great Exhibition – Hyde Park, Lond.

Showed Britain's indust. achievement. Iron + glass –

3 storeys, 3 times length of St Paul's Cath.

Gt Exhib huge success – 14,000 exhibitors

fr. 32 countries – 6 mill. visitors.

Exhib ended – what to do with bldg?

Pulled down, rebuilt in S. London –

now 5 storeys. Called 'The People's Palace'.

Ord'ry people came for entertainment –

fountains + sculpture collection.

1883 – concert hall inside, 3 theatres.

But never made profit.

1936 – fire. Mostly destroyed.

- **Discuss the features of notes with a partner.**
- **Think of three questions about the Crystal Palace. Write them in note form.**

  1. _____

  2. _____

  3. _____

- **Swap questions with your partner. Can you understand each other's notes? Discuss any problems you have.**

Now try this!

- **Work with a partner. Take turns to tell each other about somewhere you have visited.**
- **Make brief notes on your partner's talk.**
- **Form a group. Tell the group about where your partner went.**

Teachers' note Give each child a copy of this page. Discuss that note-taking varies depending on content and purpose (for example, listening to extended presentations; making notes on content, style and points to question). Revise various methods of doing this. Discuss the difference between making notes for yourself to refer to, and making notes for someone else to understand.

Developing Literacy
Speaking & Listening
Year 6
© A & C BLACK

Note it!

- **Listen to the speech about how surnames came about.**
  Make notes in the bubbles.

Why were people given surnames?

List the different ways surnames were chosen.

How could surnames be used as a kind of address?

Why might a father and son have different surnames?

- **Compare your notes with a partner's.**
  Whose notes do you think are clearer?
  Discuss the differences between them.

Surnames

Surnames were introduced in the Middle Ages to distinguish between people with the same first name. The prefix 'sur' means 'over and above', or 'additional'; so a surname was a kind of nickname used after a person's first name. Surnames sometimes described a physical feature of the person (such as Longshanks) or the job he did (such as Smith or Wright). A smith was a man who worked with metal, and a wright was someone who made things from wood. The name Baker speaks for itself, but a female baker was called a Baxter.

Many names were borrowed from geographical features and were used as a kind of address. If a man called William lived by a river or stream, he might be known as William River or William Brook. This is where the names Field, Dale and Hill came from.

People in the same family could have different surnames. For example, if a man called John thatched roofs, he would probably be known as John the Thatcher, but his eldest son might have the surname Johnson. Another of his sons might be called John the Younger. In Ireland the prefix 'O' meant 'son of', as did 'Mac' in Scotland. 'Fitz' comes from an old word meaning 'son of'.

Teachers' note Do not allow the children to read the passage (cut along the dotted line or mask the passage before photocopying). Ensure that the children read the headings in the bubbles before you read the passage to them. Encourage them to listen carefully and make notes.

Developing Literacy
Speaking & Listening
Year 6
© A & C BLACK

A Scottish ballad

- **Listen to this ballad. It uses Scottish dialect words.**
- **Underline in red the** | dialect | **words.**
- **Underline in blue the words that sound almost the same as standard English words.**

The Twa* Corbies*

As I was walking all alane,
I heard twa corbies making a mane*;
The tane unto the tither did say,
'Whar sall we gang and dine the day?' –

'In behint yon auld fail dyke*
I wot there lies a new-slain knight;
And naebody kens that he lies there
But his hawk, his hound, and his lady fair.

'His hound is to the hunting gane,
His hawk to fetch the wild-fowl hame,
His lady's ta'en anither mate,
So we may mak' our dinner sweet.'

'Mony a one for him maks mane,
But nane sall ken whar he is gane:
O'er his white banes, where they are bare,
The wind sall blaw for evermair.'

                                    Anonymous

***twa** two
***corbies** crows
***mane** noise
***fail dyke** bank of turf

- **Practise performing the poem with a partner. One of you should read the first and last verses. The other should read the middle two verses.**
- **If the poem was in standard English, would it be less effective? Discuss this with your partner.**

- **Look in poetry books for another poem written in dialect.**
- **Prepare a performance of it, on your own or with a partner.**

Teachers' note Read the poem aloud for the children just to listen to, then read it again verse by verse, allowing time for them to underline the words. They may need help with other unfamiliar words, such as 'wot' (know) and 'kens' (knows). The children will need access to poetry books for the extension activity. Allow opportunities for them to perform the poems to the class.

Developing Literacy
Speaking & Listening
Year 6
© A & C BLACK

Talk proper!

- **Work in a group. Cut out the cards.**
- **Take turns to pick a card and read out the sentence. Talk about who the speaker and audience might be.**

Is the sentence formal or informal?

I'd like a lemonade please.	Catch you later, mate.
Refreshments are served in the hall.	Oi, give us a crisp!
We simply do not have sufficient resources.	Excuse me, are you going to the town centre?
Hang on, I'll just ask Em.	Be quiet, please!

Now try this!

- **In your group, role-play a scene where someone uses informal language in a formal situation.**

How could you make it funny?

What will happen next?

Teachers' note Split the class into groups of four and give each group a copy of this page. Discuss that different situations call for different kinds of language – formal or informal. Use examples from school to highlight when it is appropriate to use formal and informal language (for example, speaking to the headteacher/speaking in the playground).

**Developing Literacy
Speaking & Listening
Year 6
© A & C BLACK**

27

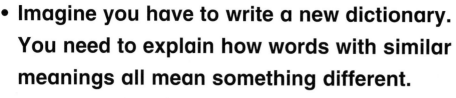

The same but different

- Imagine you have to write a new dictionary. You need to explain how words with similar meanings all mean something different.
- In your group, decide who will research each set of words.
- Research your words, then tell the group about them.
- The group should ask questions and give their own ideas.

Use a dictionary and a thesaurus to help.

DICTIONARY

THESAURUS

A

firm
obstinate
pig-headed

B

rare
unique
odd

C

witty
funny
brilliant

D

news
rumour
scandal

E

anger
irritation
fury

F

stroll
wander
ramble

Now try this!

- In your group, choose one of the sets of words.
- Make a poster showing the similarities and differences in meaning.

Discuss how you will present the information.

Teachers' note The children should work in groups of up to six. (It does not matter if some sets of words are not researched.) Make enough copies of this page for the children to refer to. They will need access to a range of dictionaries and, if possible, the Internet.

Developing Literacy Speaking & Listening Year 6 © A & C BLACK

Firework sense

- **Work in a group. You are going to plan a presentation on how to use fireworks safely.**
- **Read the rules for using fireworks. Discuss the reason for each rule and make notes on the chart.**

Rule	Reason for rule
1. Keep fireworks in a closed box.	
2. Follow the instructions on each firework carefully.	
3. Light the end of the fuse at arm's length.	
4. Never return to a firework once it has been lit.	
5. Keep pets indoors.	
6. Never put fireworks in your pocket.	
7. Never throw or play with fireworks.	

- **Now plan your presentation. Will you use pictures and sound effects? How will you share out the talking?**
- **Rehearse your presentation, then give it to the rest of the class.**

Now try this!

- **Listen to other people's comments on your presentation. Make some notes about how you could improve the content and style.**

Teachers' note Split the class into groups of three to four and give each group a copy of this page. One child in the group should act as scribe. Encourage members of the group to offer constructive criticism of one another's ideas, and to respond in appropriate ways.

**Developing Literacy
Speaking & Listening
Year 6
© A & C BLACK**

Recycling plastic

- **Work in a group of four.**
- **Cut out the cards and take one each. Each card explains one stage in the process of recycling plastic.**
- **Explain your part of the process to the others in your group.**
- **As a group, decide on the correct order. Then plan the whole explanation.**

Strings of plastic are cooled in water. When solid, revolving cutter chops them into tiny pieces (pellets). Pellets bagged and sold to a factory – made into other things.

Recycling machine opens bags of old plastic. Plastic goes through granulator → smaller flakes (granules).

Plastic granules are dried. Machine called an 'extruder' melts plastic and forces it through small holes – comes out as a kind of string.

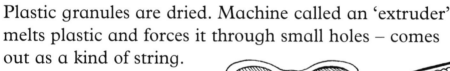

Recycling machine washes plastic granules – removes paper label and any dirt (some old plastic comes from rubbish dumps).

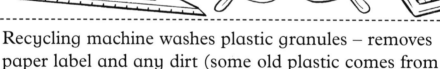

Now try this!

- **On another piece of paper, draw a design made from 2-D shapes.**
- **Describe the design for your partner to draw.**
- **Compare your partner's drawing with your own. Discuss how well you explained it.**

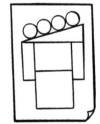

Teachers' note Split the class into groups of four and give each group a copy of this page. The children should work through the process as a group, questioning each other until they understand how plastic is recycled. In the extension activity, the children need to keep their drawing hidden from their partner. They will need to use mathematical vocabulary relating to shapes and position.

Developing Literacy
Speaking & Listening
Year 6
© A & C BLACK

Back to front

- **Work in a group of four. Read the sentences.**
- **Work out what they have in common.**

Too bad, I hid a boot.	Step on no pets.
Ten animals I slam in a net.	War, sir, is raw.

- **Shade each strip below in a different colour.**
  Then cut along the dotted lines.
- **Put the words in the correct order to make sentences**
  like those above.

A	A	A	A	A
more	a	Roman	yawn	way

B	B	B	B	B
pew	a	panic	in	we

C	C	C	C
to	sir	rise	vote

D	D	D	D	D	D
star	live	on	evil	no	rats

E	E	E	E	E
is	it	Simon	Miss	no

F	F	F	F	F	F
ate	my	worm	metal	Mr	Owl

Teachers' note Split the class into groups of four and give each group a copy of this page. Groups can be formed so that children who will find this more difficult are given support. Encourage the children to look closely at the letters of the words to find out what the sentences have in common. The children will need coloured pencils.

Developing Literacy
Speaking & Listening
Year 6
© A & C BLACK

True or false?

- **Work in a group of six. Cut out the cards.**
- **On your own, pick a card and decide whether you agree with the statement.**
- **Then explain to your group why you think the statement is true or false. Give examples.**
- **Listen to your friends' ideas on the topic and reply to them.**

Eating a balanced diet helps you to work better at school.

Honesty is always the best policy.

Children who behave badly at school should be given extra homework.

People were happier in the past.

The number 13 is unlucky.

Watching television is a waste of time.

Now try this!

- **In your group, try to agree which statements are true and which are false.**

Do you think you could prove the statements? How?

Teachers' note Split the class into groups of up to six and give each group a copy of this page. Stress that there are no right or wrong answers. Encourage the children to listen to one another's ideas and to find ways of coping with disagreements to reach a consensus. During the plenary, talk about the type of language used when trying to resolve disagreements.

**Developing Literacy
Speaking & Listening
Year 6
© A & C BLACK**

Rescue mission

This hot-air balloon is losing power. Only one person can stay in the basket, otherwise the balloon will crash-land.

• **Decide who you would choose to save.**

schoolgirl

postal worker

firefighter

nurse

charity worker

• **Note down the reasons why you would save this person and not the others.**

I would save _____ .

Reasons _____

_____

_____

• **Now work in a group. Try to agree on which person to save.**

Teachers' note Give each child a copy of the sheet. Allow five minutes for the children, working individually, to decide which person they would like to save, and list their reasons. Then split the class into groups of four to five. Allow each group to work out for themselves how they will decide which passenger to save.

**Developing Literacy
Speaking & Listening
Year 6
© A & C BLACK**

Phone talk

- **Work in a group of four. Cut out the cards.**
- **Pick a card and read the role-play situation. Plan what you will say.**
- **Role-play the conversation with a partner. Ask the others in your group to listen and to comment on the language you use.**

Is the situation formal or informal?

A

Phone your friend's mum to apologise for breaking one of her kitchen plates. Explain how it happened and offer to pay for a new one. Explain that you won't be able to pay until you have saved up your pocket money.

B

Phone a lady who is advertising a cheap bike in the local newspaper. Ask what it is like and find out why it is cheap. Arrange a time to collect and pay for the bike. Ask for directions to her house.

C

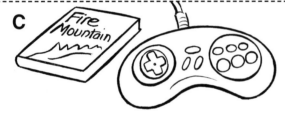

Phone a friend who is selling a computer game. Ask questions to check that it is the one you want. Talk about the price. Arrange where and when you will meet to pay for the game.

D

Phone the police. It is midnight and you think someone is breaking into the house next door. Give information about what you can see and hear. Explain how to get there.

Now try this!

- **Role-play the conversation again using the opposite style of language.**

Change formal to informal and vice versa.

- **Discuss with your group why this style of language is not appropriate.**

Teachers' note Split the class into groups of four and give each group a copy of this page. Before beginning, discuss how and why spoken language varies. In the extension activity, explain that only the person initiating the conversation should change their style of language, and the other person should use the same style as before; this will help them to see why the language is inappropriate.

**Developing Literacy
Speaking & Listening
Year 6
© A & C BLACK**

Changing audience

- **Read the newspaper report.**

Builder trapped in wall collapse

Brave firefighters and ambulance personnel yesterday fought to free a builder trapped when a steel girder fell on him.

The builder, called Mark Roberts, aged 32, was renovating Barts Shoe Shop in Heppenstall High Street when the wall collapsed and he was trapped.

Mr Roberts was taken to the local hospital and is said to be out of danger and progressing well.

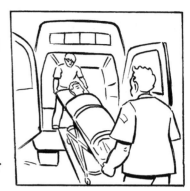

- **With a partner, read out Mrs Roberts' speech bubbles.**

- **Discuss who you think she is speaking to in each speech bubble. How can you tell?**

A I'm sorry, Mark can't make his appointment tomorrow. He's had an accident at work. Can I rearrange it please?

B An' so I ran down the ginnel an' there's all these fire engines. My heart was in me mouth! An' there's Mark on a stretcher, white as a sheet.

C It's all right, love. Everything's OK. We'll go an' see 'im later and take a big box o' chocs.

D I would like to thank you all for helping to save my husband. Mark and I are both really grateful.

Now try this!

- **Role-play these situations with a partner. Think about what kind of language is appropriate.**

A You are Mark Roberts telling your sister about what happened.

B You are one of the firefighters reporting the event to your boss.

C You are a witness telling the story to a newspaper reporter.

Teachers' note Give each pair a copy of this page. Before beginning, remind the children that spoken language varies according to context and purpose, drawing out the idea that people naturally alter the way in which they speak depending on the audience. During the plenary, discuss the differences between formal and informal speech.

Developing Literacy Speaking & Listening Year 6 © A & C BLACK

Camera... action!

- **Work with a partner. Cut out the cards.**
- **Imagine you are the directors of a spy film. Put the pictures in order to tell a story.**
- **Try changing the order. Decide which is the best.**

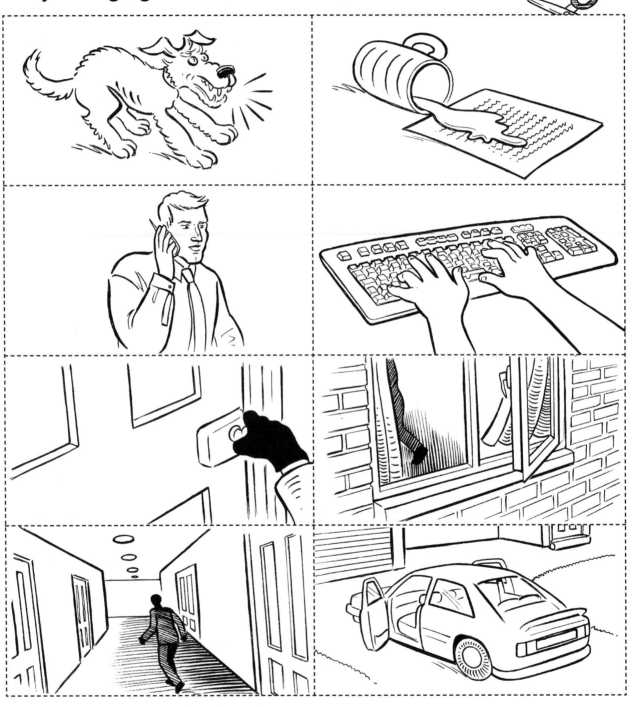

- **With your partner, practise acting out your story. Make it as exciting as you can.**

Teachers' note Give each pair a copy of this page. Stress that the pictures can be interpreted and sequenced in a variety of ways. Invite pairs to act out their story, and highlight the variety of different stories they have made. Talk about how different pairs built tension in different ways. You could ask the class to vote on which performance was the most dramatic.

Developing Literacy Speaking & Listening Year 6 © A & C BLACK

Character lines

- **Complete this sheet to help you comment on the characters in a play or film.**

Title of play/film _____

Names of main characters

_____

_____

_____

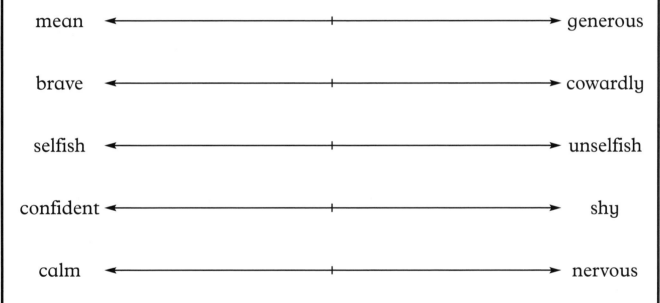

- **On each line, show how far you think the characters match either of the adjectives. Mark a cross for each character and label it with their initials.**

mean   ⟵————————————+————————————⟶   generous

brave   ⟵————————————+————————————⟶   cowardly

selfish   ⟵————————————+————————————⟶   unselfish

confident   ⟵————————————+————————————⟶   shy

calm   ⟵————————————+————————————⟶   nervous

- **Discuss your choices with a partner. Explain how you know what the characters are like.**

Now try this!

- **Draw three more character lines and label them with opposite adjectives. Mark the same characters on these lines.**
- **Note down things the characters do or say which helped you decide.**

Teachers' note The children should first watch a recorded or live performance, or a suitable short piece of video. Model how to complete the character lines using a character from a book they have recently read. Discuss whether the children change their minds about characters during the course of a play or film, and why.

Developing Literacy
Speaking & Listening
Year 6
© A & C BLACK

Character detective

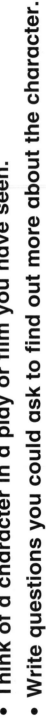

- Think of a character in a play or film you have seen.
- Write questions you could ask to find out more about the character.
- Then write what you think the answers would be. Say why you think that.

Title of play/film _____

Character _____

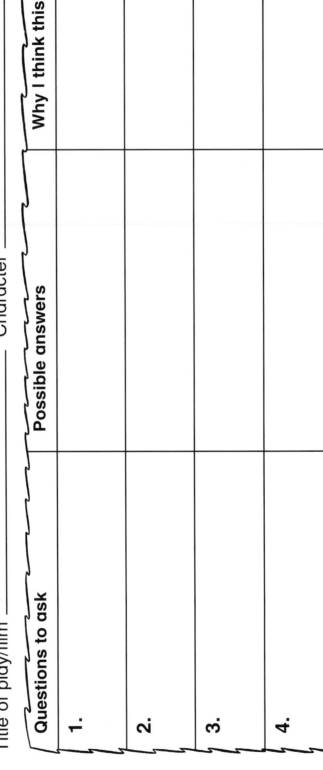

Questions to ask	Possible answers	Why I think this
1.		
2.		
3.		
4.		

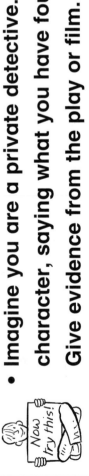

Now try this!

- Imagine you are a private detective. Write a report about the character, saying what you have found out about him or her. Give evidence from the play or film.

Teachers' note The children should first watch a recorded or live performance. Encourage them to think about what the character says and does, and how this can help them to decide what the answers to their questions might be. During the plenary, invite children to suggest different possible answers to the questions.

Developing Literacy
**Speaking & Listening
Year 6**
© A & C BLACK

Tense moments

Writers use │ tension │ to make
their plays or films exciting.

- Use this sheet to make notes
  about moments of tension in
  a play or film you have seen.

Writers can build tension by
keeping the audience, or one of
the characters, in suspense.

Title of play/film _____

Moments of tension – what happens?	How does the writer make this even more exciting?

Now try this!

- Make up another scene which involves the same
  characters. Think about how you
  can create a moment of tension.
- Write a short playscript of the scene.
  Remember to use stage directions.

Kate (standing up
suddenly): We
must leave at
once.

Teachers' note This activity could be used as a follow-up to page 38. The children should first watch
a recorded or live performance. Discuss with the class what might constitute a moment of tension: for
example, something might go wrong, or characters might have an argument. For the extension activity,
the children may need reminding how to set out a playscript.

**Developing Literacy
Speaking & Listening
Year 6
© A & C BLACK**

39

Film of the book

- **Watch a film based on a book you have read.**
- **Complete this sheet to help you comment on the film.**

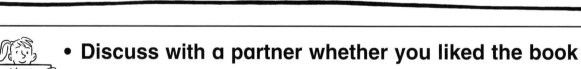

Title of book _____

Author _____

Were the characters in the film how you imagined them?

Was anything left out? What? Why?

Was anything added? What? Why?

Did the film director change the book in other ways? How?

Did you agree with the changes? Why/why not?

Now try this!

- **Discuss with a partner whether you liked the book or the film more. Explain why.**

Teachers' note For this activity the children need to watch a film of a book they have read. Children who find the activity difficult could work with a partner to produce a joint sheet.

Developing Literacy
Speaking & Listening
Year 6
© A & C BLACK

Character alley

• **Use this activity to explore a scene in a book you have read.**

Title of book _____   Author _____

Chapter/page number _____   Main character _____

☆ One person is going to play the part of the main character and walk down the 'alley'.

☆ Imagine you are another character in the scene. You are going to give your character's opinion of the main character as he or she walks past.

• **Plan what you are going to say. You could use the sentence starters in the speech bubbles.**

Character whose opinion I am giving _____

I think you are

I think you should

I feel

You are

• **Now you have heard everyone's opinions, have you learned anything new about the character? Talk to a partner.**

Teachers' note Choose a character and scene from a book the whole class has read, and fill this in at the top of the page before photocopying. After writing in the speech bubbles, the children should form two lines facing each other, with a small gap or 'alley' between the rows. The character moves down the alley and each child in turn speaks to the character (who remains silent).

**Developing Literacy
Speaking & Listening
Year 6
© A & C BLACK**

Freeze!

- Work in a group. Choose a passage from a book and re-read it together.
- Act a | freeze frame | for each main event.
- Sketch your freeze frames here.
  Write a sentence to describe each one.

1.

2.

3.

4.

- In your group, act each freeze frame again.
  In role, take turns to explain to the others what your character is thinking and feeling at that moment.

Now try this!

Teachers' note This activity could be used with the passage from *Oliver Twist* on page 45, or with another story the children have read. Help them to choose a suitable scene involving several characters. Explain that in a freeze frame the action of the drama is frozen, like a photograph.

Developing Literacy
Speaking & Listening
Year 6
© A & C BLACK

In the hot seat

- **Use this activity to explore a character in a book.**

Title of book _____

Author _____ Character _____

☆ One person is going to imagine they are the character and sit in the 'hot seat'.

☆ Think of questions to ask the character in the hot seat.

Why did you...?

What would you do if...?

- **Plan your questions. Write in the speech bubbles.**

- **With a partner, discuss how the character answered your questions. How would you answer the questions differently?**

Teachers' note Choose a character from a book all the children have read. First sit in a circle and together briefly recap what happens in the book, making sure that all children have the chance to contribute. Provide one chair (the 'hot seat') and ask for a volunteer to take on the role of the character. The other children should plan and write questions to ask the character.

**Developing Literacy
Speaking & Listening
Year 6
© A & C BLACK**

Speak your mind

- **Choose an important moment in a book you are reading.**
- **Imagine you are one of the characters. What are you thinking and feeling? Write your ideas here.**

Title of book _____ Page number _____

Author_____ Character _____

I am thinking _____

_____

_____

because

_____

_____

_____

_____

_____

_____

 *Now try this!*

I am feeling

_____

_____

_____

_____

_____

_____

_____

because _____

_____

_____

- **Work in a group. Ask the others to say what they think your character is thinking and feeling at that moment.**
- **Discuss different ideas.**

Teachers' note Use this activity with a text you are reading as a class, and together decide on the important moment that will be the focus of the activity. Once the children have completed the activity sheet, move among the group inviting the children to speak in turn (for example, by lightly touching them on the shoulder).

**Developing Literacy
Speaking & Listening
Year 6
© A & C BLACK**

I want some more...

In this passage from *Oliver Twist*, Oliver plucks up the courage to ask for more food at the workhouse.

- **Read the passage.**

The evening arrived; the boys took their places. The master, in his cook's uniform, stationed himself at the copper*; his pauper* assistants ranged themselves behind him; the gruel* was served out; and a long grace was said over the short commons*. The gruel disappeared; the boys whispered to each other, and winked at Oliver; while his next neighbours nudged him. Child as he was, he was desperate with hunger, and reckless with misery. He rose from the table; and advancing to the master, basin and spoon in hand, said: somewhat alarmed at his own temerity:

　'Please, sir, I want some more.'

　The master was a fat, healthy man; but he turned very pale. He gazed in stupefied astonishment on the small rebel for some seconds, and then clung for support to the copper.

　'What!' said the master at length, in a faint voice.

　'Please, sir,' replied Oliver, 'I want some more.'

　The master aimed a blow at Oliver's head with the ladle; pinioned him in his arms; and shrieked aloud for the beadle*.

From *Oliver Twist* by Charles Dickens

> *copper** large copper cooking pot
> *pauper** poor boy
> *gruel** tasteless porridge
> *short commons** small amount of food
> *beadle** the person in charge of the workhouse

- **With a partner, write a playscript of the scene to perform to younger children.**

First talk about:

☆ how to set out a playscript

☆ what you need to leave out

☆ what you need to put in or change to help the audience understand it

☆ how you will show what the characters are thinking and feeling.

- **Perform your playscript.**
- **Ask your audience what they thought was good about your performance.**

Teachers' note Read the passage to the children and discuss what they know about the Victorian workhouse system and why Oliver acts as he does. The children will need to think about how to adapt the scene for younger children: for example, by changing the language and replacing unfamiliar terms. The playscripts could be performed to a mixed audience of younger children and the rest of the class.

Developing Literacy
Speaking & Listening
Year 6
© A & C BLACK

What a performance!

This poem is full of sound words. You are going to prepare a performance of it for parents.

- **Work in a group. Read the poem. Underline the words that you will stress when you perform it.**

The Blacksmiths

Swart swarthy smiths besmattered with smoke
Drive me to death with din of their dints.
Such noise on nights heard no one never;
What knavish cry and clattering of knocks!
The snub nosed changelings cry after 'col, col!'
And blow their bellows till all their brains burst:
'Huf, puf!' says one; 'haf, paf' another.
They spit and sprawl and spell many spells;
They grind teeth and gnash them, and groan together,
And hold them hot with their hard hammers.
Of bull's hide are their leather aprons.
Their shanks are shielded from the fierce sparks;
Heavy hammers they have; that are hard handled,
Stark strokes they strike on an anvil of steel
Lus, bus! Las, das! They strike in rotation:
The Devil destroy such a doleful noise.
The master lengthens a little piece, belabours a smaller,
Twines the two together, strikes a treble note
Tik, tak! Hic, hac! Ticket, tacket! Tyk, tak!

Anonymous

- **Which words make the sounds made by blacksmiths? List them.** _____

_____

- **Practise performing the poem with sound effects and actions.**

Now try this!

- **Think of another job or activity that makes a lot of noise. Write a short poem about it.**
- **Practise performing your poem.**

Include **onomatopoeic** (sound) words.

Teachers' note Split the class into groups of three to four. Each child will need a copy of this page. Read the poem with the children and explain that it was written a long time ago – probably in medieval times. Help them with words they find unfamiliar or difficult. In groups, they should decide how they are going to share out different parts of the poem.

Developing Literacy Speaking & Listening Year 6 © A & C BLACK

- **Read the poem.**

The Muddy, Mucky, Murky Mouch

On a small asteroid
in the terrible void
dwells a filthy old slouch,
the vile m-m-m-Mouch.
   He sleeps in spaghetti,
looks just like a yeti,
and his grotty green wig
would embarrass a pig.
   He enjoys a good splosh
in tomato juice squash,
while from swimming in sludge
he's the colour of fudge.
   He gobbles green gottles,
swigs pond ooze from bottles
and the stench of his breath
scares all known germs to death.
   He's a jumbo-sized pest,
falls asleep fully dressed,
and far, far out in Space
he's the last of his race.
   The vile m-m-m-Mouch
doesn't run, jump or crouch,
but squats, gnarled as a gnome,
on his asteroid home.

Wes Magee

- **With a partner, underline the words you like the sound of.**
- **Think about how you will perform the poem to a group of young children.**

Which parts will you stress?

How will you make it fun for your audience?

Now try this!

- **Imagine you meet the creature in the poem. With a partner, role-play a conversation. Make up your own sound words.**

Teachers' note The children should work in pairs. Remind them that their performance is for younger children, and ask them to think about how they make it fun. Discuss that many of the words use alliteration, and these are the words they should be making most dramatic.

**Developing Literacy
Speaking & Listening
Year 6
© A & C BLACK**

How did you do?

Name _____ **Date** _____

Activity title _____

When you listened to others

- **What was good about what they said?**

  _____

  _____

- **What could they have done better?**

  _____

  _____

When you spoke

- **What did you do well?**

  _____

  _____

- **What could you do better next time?**

  _____

  _____

When you talked in a group

- **What was good about your discussion?**

  _____

  _____

- **Did you have any problems? If you did, what were they?**

  _____

  _____

Teachers' note Photocopy this page and fill in the title of the activity to be self-assessed. Before the children complete the assessment sheet, you could ask them whether they enjoyed the activity, and to explain why or why not.

Developing Literacy
Speaking & Listening
Year 6
© A & C BLACK